THE ARCHITECTURE AND INFRASTRUCTURE OF BRITAIN'S RAILWAYS

Eastern and Southern England

Patrick Bennett

AMBERLEY

First published 2018

Amberley Publishing
The Hill, Stroud
Gloucestershire, GL5 4EP

www.amberley-books.com

Copyright © Patrick Bennett, 2018

The right of Patrick Bennett to be identified as
the Author of this work has been asserted in
accordance with the Copyrights, Designs and
Patents Act 1988.

ISBN 978 1 4456 8149 8 (print)
ISBN 978 1 4456 8150 4 (ebook)

British Library Cataloguing in Publication Data.
A catalogue record for this book is available from
the British Library.

Origination by Amberley Publishing.
Printed in the UK.

Contents

Introduction

British railway stations show a considerable variety in their construction. This variety depends to a large extent on the era in which they were constructed, so that for example those built in the mid-nineteenth century tend to have a more restrained classical style than those built towards the end, when Victorian Gothic was at its height. In between there were many other styles, which included Tudor, *cottage orné* and so-called 'Jacobethan' and 'Wrenaissance'. The twentieth century brought its own influences, particularly notable being the art deco of the interwar years. Size varied enormously as well, from the humble wayside halt with, at best, a tiny shelter, to the magnificence of a city centre terminus.

The railways were not just concerned with the carriage of passengers and, indeed, in terms of revenue, freight traffic was far more important for many companies. To support this traffic vast goods depots, warehouses and granaries were constructed in the major cities, while in the country every station had its goods shed of varying size and style. Needed too were weighbridges, cranes, hoists and lifts. Construction of the railways involved civil engineering on a scale never seen before, with the building of viaducts, tunnels and bridges of various types, a selection of which are shown here.

Signal boxes and signals are perhaps one of the most characteristic aspects of the railway scene. The area of Britain that this book covers was particularly rich in traditional signalling at the time these photographs were taken. Sadly, nearly all the signal boxes and signals depicted here have now been replaced by modern signalling centres.

Other buildings provided for the railways included hotels, locomotive depots, accommodation of various kinds for railway employees and of course the great works, where engines and carriages were constructed and maintained. Also included in this volume are the small details that were such a familiar part of the everyday backdrop, including signs from different eras, lamps, benches, barrows and trolleys, footbridges and various architectural details.

Many railway buildings are of considerable architectural or historical interest, sometimes both. Historic England has a system of classifying such buildings as follows: Grade I – buildings of exceptional interest; Grade II* – particularly important buildings of more than special interest; Grade II – buildings of special interest.

This volume also contains the work of other photographers and the author and publisher would like to thank the following for permission to use copyright material in this book: Fin Fahey for the photograph taken at North Woolwich, Ben Brooksbank for the photograph taken at Fenchurch Street, Martyn Davies for the photograph taken at Leatherhead, Steve Keiretsu for the photograph taken at Surbiton, Perryman for the photograph taken at Waterloo, Edwardx for the photograph taken at Kew Bridge, and Cupcakekid for the photograph taken at Clayton Tunnel.

Patrick Bennett
Millay, France
June 2018

Stations

The Midland Railway

The Midland Counties Railway opened its line from Derby to Rugby in 1840. Loughborough was one of the first stations, though the present building dates from 1872. Its most notable features are the cast-iron and glass, ridge and furrow platform canopies. Of particular note is the delicate filigree work in the canopy trusses and column brackets. Grade II listed.

Leicester station was rebuilt in 1892 to the design of Charles Trubshaw. Constructed of red brick, the frontage screen is dressed with bands and mouldings of pale terracotta tiles. The porte cochère has separate openings for arrivals and departures. At one end is a hexagonal clock tower, and a parapet surmounted by urns extends the full length of the frontage. Grade II listed.

The Midland Railway, successor to the MCR, completed a line from Leicester to Hitchin in 1858. At Market Harborough it met the LNW, which had reached the town seven years earlier. In 1884 a joint station was constructed. Built in a pleasing style, sometimes known as Queen Anne, or even 'Wrenaissance', it is a brick-built structure with stone pilasters and door and window mouldings. The hipped roof has a number of elegant chimney stacks. Grade II listed.

Glendon & Rushton is a superb example of a small MR station. It is built of limestone with brick chimney stacks and window and door arches in contrasting coloured brick. Very typical of the MR are the wavy bargeboards and the lozenge-pattern window ironwork. Originally named Rushton, the station was opened with the line in 1857. It was renamed Glendon & Rushton in 1896 and closed in 1960. Grade II listed.

With a distinct family likeness to Glendon & Rushton, but on a larger scale and built of brick, is Wellingborough. Contrasting-coloured brick is used for the window arches and also for the blind arcade. The slate roof has a dentilled cornice in pale brick. Once again we see the lozenge windows and wavy bargeboards. The architect was C. H. Driver. Grade II listed.

Rushden station is the site of the Rushden, Higham & Wellingborough Railway. Situated on the Wellingborough–Higham Ferrers branch, which opened in 1893, the station lost its passenger service in 1959. Built of red brick with a plinth in contrasting blue brick, the station has been preserved intact. The preservation group aims to complete a tourist line from Rushden to Higham Ferrers.

Situated on the Nottingham–Lincoln line and opened in 1846, Newark Castle station is built in the restrained classical style of the mid-nineteenth century. It is a single-storey building constructed of buff brick with stone pilasters, plinth, cornice, and door and window dressings. Disused when this photograph was taken in 1990, it has now been partially returned to railway use. Grade II listed.

Italianate in style, Collingham is built of gault brick with contrasting red brick in the arches of the arcade and windows. Ashlar has been used for sills, keystones and cornice. Since this photograph was taken in 1989, the building has become a much-improved private dwelling, listed as Grade II. Of particular note is that the boxed-in pediment on the projecting bay has been restored.

Stamford originally had both a GNR and an MR station. Stamford East, the GNR station, closed in 1957, and Stamford Town, the MR station, was proposed for closure in the Beeching report. Happily it did not close, because it is an architectural gem. Dating from 1848, it was originally built for the Syston & Peterborough Railway, later part of the MR. It is constructed of grey limestone in a loosely Tudor style. Of special note are the platform canopies in two different styles, and the hexagonal turret. Grade II listed.

Rowsley station came into being as a result of the Manchester, Buxton, Matlock & Midland Junction Railway's drive towards Manchester, which, reaching Rowsley in 1849, got no further for another fourteen years. When the line was eventually extended to Buxton a new station was built and the original became redundant. It continued as a goods facility until the closure of the line in 1967. The photograph dates from 1989, when the building was in a sorry state. Since then it has been restored and is now part of a shopping complex, Grade II.

London & North Western Railway

Hard to believe but the station building at Oundle was left to rot after the Peterborough–Northampton line closed to all traffic in 1972. Built in 1845 to the design of J. W. Livock, the building is constructed of limestone ashlar with a slate roof. The platform side, seen here, has three gables, the centre one of which has an oriel window. The two flanking gables have dripstones and the windows on the ground floor have mullions and transoms. Happily the building has survived and has been restored, and is Grade II listed.

The three LNW stations featured here share the same fate – they are all closed. Wakerley & Barrowden was on the stretch of line between Yarwell Junction and Seaton, opened in 1879. The line here was on an embankment. The platform buildings are of lapped-boarded timber sitting on a plain brick base. The stationmaster's house is also of plain brick, relieved by string courses and plinth in a darker colour.

Further to the west on the line to Rugby is the station of Rockingham. Built of coursed limestone rubble with ashlar dressings, it is unusual in having the station name painted on the wall. The station closed in 1966.

Great Northern Railway

Looking at this photograph of Stixwould today, it is hard to believe that this was once the main line between London and York. The Lincolnshire Loop line was opened by the GNR in 1848 only to be superseded by the direct east coast route two years later. All that remains of the station is the stationmaster's house and the signal box, which have been linked with a sympathetic extension. Both are built of brick in Flemish bond, while the house has stone lintels and sills. Note the typical GNR decorative bargeboards and finials on both the signal box and house.

Further south on the Loop line is Tattershall. This section of line closed in 1963. The station building here, constructed in buff brick, is attributed to Joseph Cubitt and dates from *c.* 1847. It is a sympathetic three-storey building in an Italianate style. Of particular note are the soaring chimney stacks. Grade II listed.

Nottingham London Road Low Level. This extraordinary building was constructed in 1857 for the Ambergate, Nottingham, Boston & Eastern Junction Railway to the design of Thomas Hine. It is built of red brick with ashlar dressings, parapet and balcony, has a French style gable and turret and a stone and cast-iron porte cochère. The last passenger train ran in 1944 but the station continued to handle goods until the 1980s. It is currently a health club and is Grade II listed.

The GNR went to no great expense in building its intermediate stations, which are mostly modest single-storey buildings in buff brick, as here at Huntingdon. It was constructed in 1850 to the design of Henry Goddard. Grade II listed.

St Neot's is another single-storey building of no great merit, but is pleasant enough. The buff brick is relieved by contrasting door and window arches, plinth and string course. The next station south of Huntingdon, it was also opened in 1850.

St Alban's London Road preceded the MR station by some ten years. It was opened by the GNR in 1865 as the terminus of its branch from Hatfield. Passenger traffic ceased in 1951 and freight in 1964. A completely symmetrical building of two gables joined by a third, it is built of red brick with flint facings on the ground floor. When this photograph was taken in 1990 the building was in use as a scrapyard. It has subsequently become a business centre and is situated in the middle of a new housing development.

Spalding station consists of a motley collection of one-, two- and three-storey buildings built of pale brick with painted stone dressings. It was built in 1848 for the GNR but in 1882 it became a joint GER/GNR station. Today, simply a through station, Spalding was once the meeting place of lines from six different directions. Grade II listed.

Great Central Railway

Kirton Lindsey station came into being with the opening of the Manchester, Sheffield & Lincolnshire's Sheffield–Grimsby line. It is built of both buff and red brick with stone quoins, string course, and window and door dressings. It has retained its impressive array of original chimney stacks. The station sees just three return trains on Saturdays only, running between Sheffield and Cleethorpes, and is Grade II listed.

Barnetby is at the junction of lines from Lincoln, Gainsborough and Scunthorpe. The line from Market Rasen arrived first, followed by the Gainsborough line. Finally, in 1866 the line to Scunthorpe and beyond came into being. The station building is in red brick and mostly undistinguished apart from its unusual broken pediments.

Brocklesby was built for the MS&L in 1847. It is constructed of red brick in Flemish bond, with ashlar dressings, in a style sometimes known as 'Jacobethan'. Its splendour is owed to the fact that it was the home station of the Earl of Yarborough, who lived at Brocklesby Hall, and who was chairman of the MSL at the time of its construction. Lord Yarborough and his guests had their own private waiting room in the station. Grade II listed.

Habrough sits at the junction of the lines to Cleethorpes and to New Holland. The station consists of a pair of gables joined by a glazed screen sheltering the passenger area. It is of brick in English bond with a slate roof and plain bargeboards.

Nearer to Cleethorpes is Great Coates. Much modified and now a private house, it consists of three gables with a small canopy filling the angle between them. It is constructed of brick with ashlar quoins and dressings, and a ball finial atop each gable. The ground-floor windows have been much modified.

Howsham provides a better example of the MSL standard design as it has been much less modified. It also has an extension. Note that the column supporting the canopy is quite elaborate with a decorative spandrel. The bay window may not be original. Like all the stations between Lincoln and Barnetby, apart from Market Rasen, Howsham was closed in 1965 as part of the Beeching measures.

Market Rasen station was constructed in 1848 for the Great Grimsby & Sheffield Junction Railway. This is another building showing the restrained elegance of mid-nineteenth-century design. Built entirely of pale yellow brick, it has a rather naked appearance. This is due to the fact that the overall roof has been removed, to be replaced by the smallest of canopies. The square chimney stacks are a pleasing feature, though one has been extended using a different coloured brick. Grade II listed.

Not every station is so elegant. This is Ulceby, which despite sitting at the junction of four lines has the barest minimum of facilities – just a single wooden platform for trains in both directions and a shelter, not even on the platform. The single line leading to the left is to Cleethorpes, and the pair of lines on the right are for Barnetby. Points to note are the running-in board in original BR(ER) blue and the signal box and crossing gates. The GCR Type 5 box was demolished in 2016 and the signalling and crossing was automated.

Goxhill on the New Holland/Barton line is another MSL station to the pattern of Howsham and Great Coates. There are detail differences, however: the canopy has a sawtooth valance, a glazed screen at one end and an additional support. Note also the bell attached to one of the gables. At the time of writing the manual crossing gates shown here were still in existence.

Cleethorpes as a seaside resort was largely created by the MSL. The original station opened in 1863 but this was considerably extended in 1880–81 when the clock tower and refreshment rooms were added. Both are Grade II listed.

Deepcar is on the Great Central's Woodhead Route. It lost its passenger service as long ago as 1959 but freight trains still pass here on their way to Stocksbridge. The station buildings are constructed of coursed rubble millstone grit with ashlar quoins and dressings – a not unattractive assemblage of gables that would benefit from a thorough cleaning. The location is currently a private house.

North Eastern Railway

Goole was one of the NER's rare penetrations south of the Humber. It was opened in 1869 and it has recently been completely modernised externally, but it retains its elegant canopies, supported on cast-iron columns and decorative spandrels.

Great Eastern Railway

The GER was noted for its elegant small stations, and nowhere were they better illustrated than here at Elsenham. Much of that elegance is attributable to the canopy, with its elegant cast-iron columns, decorative spandrels and frilly valancing. Elsenham was the junction for the Thaxted branch, which closed in 1953. Grade II listed.

The next station north of Elsenham is Newport, where once again we see typical GER canopies. These date from 1885. The shape of the canopies indicate that there was once a third platform.

Continuing north we come to Audley End. The building here, dating from 1845, was designed by Francis Thompson. It is a square gault brick two-storey structure with a stucco frieze and architraves. The porte cochère is also finished in stucco. The station is actually at Wendens Ambo; the station name, and no doubt its grandeur, derive from the nearby presence of Audley End House. Audley End was the junction for the Saffron Walden branch, closed in 1964. This building is Grade II listed, as is the telephone box just glimpsed in this photograph.

Another design by Francis Thompson was Great Chesterford, just 4 miles north of Audley End. An extremely plain building, once more constructed of gault brick with stucco architraves and a deep cornice, there is an unusual, original canopy on the platform side of the building. Grade II listed.

Ely is an important junction. It has lost its branch to St Ives but there are still lines to Peterborough, King's Lynn, Norwich, Ipswich and London. The station was opened in 1843 by the Eastern Counties Railway. The frontage consists of a pair of two-storey pavilions with hidden roofs, joined by a single storey. It is constructed of buff-coloured brick with rusticated stucco on the ground floor. There are two single-storey wings.

The Lynn & Hunstanton Railway opened its line in 1862. This is one of those lines that, while not proposed for closure in the Beeching report, nevertheless did close, losing its remaining services in 1969. Halfway to Hunstanton is Dersingham. Happily the station buildings and platform canopies have survived intact. This is the Down platform.

Another lucky survivor is Lakenheath station, which sees just two trains on Saturdays, seven on Sundays, and none at all from Monday to Friday. The structures here consist of just the two shelters and the stationmaster's house. The signal box was abolished in 2012 and the line is now controlled from Cambridge. This photograph dates from 1990.

Further along the Ely–Norwich line is Thetford. This is a particularly important station architecturally as it retains features from several stages of its development. The original station was built for the Norwich & Brandon Railway in 1845. This flint-faced building can just be glimpsed beyond the red-brick structure of GER origin, built in 1889. The canopies on their elegant, cast-iron columns are also noteworthy. Grade II listed.

The East Suffolk line was proposed for closure in the Beeching report, but thanks to a vigorous local campaign it managed to survive. Woodbridge is one of the nine stations between Westerfield and Lowestoft. Designed by Frederick Barnes, it is built in buff brick with door and window dressings, and a string course in contrasting red brick.

The Yarmouth & Norwich Railway opened in 1844 and Brundall was one of the original stations. This scene will soon be no more. Under the Norwich–Yarmouth/Lowestoft resignalling project, currently underway, the manual level crossing gates and signals will go. The signals seen in the far distance at Brundall Junction will also disappear.

The magnificent edifice of Maldon station owes its elegance principally to the fact that at the time of its construction this was the prospective parliamentary seat of the deputy chairman of the ECR. Jacobean in style, it is a building of two pavilions linked by a nine-arch arcade with stucco dressings. Clever use has been made of contrasting-coloured brick to bring out architectural details. Opened in 1848, it was closed to passengers in 1964 and to freight in 1966, and it is currently in use as offices, listed as Grade II.

Histon was opened by the Wisbech, St Ives & Cambridge Junction Railway in 1847. It closed to passengers in 1970 but remained in use for freight as far as Fen Drayton until 1992, when this photograph was taken. A long campaign to reopen the railway for passenger use was unsuccessful and in the end it was decided to use the trackbed for a guided bus route, which involved the demolition of much of what can be seen here.

North Woolwich, dating from 1847, was designed by William Tite. Built of red brick, it consists of two pavilions joined by a four-bay central section, the upper storey of which is recessed. It has stucco embellishments and the two pavilions are joined by a pierced parapet. Following its closure in 2006 the station building became the site of the Great Eastern Railway Museum. Unfortunately finance to maintain the building was withdrawn and the museum closed in November 2008. The building is currently in poor condition with urgent repairs needed for the roof. Grade II listed. (Photograph by Fin Fahey)

London, Tilbury & Southend Railway

Fenchurch Street was built by the London & Blackwall Railway to the design of George Berkeley. It dates from 1834, though the zigzag canopy was a later GER replacement. Constructed of gault brick, its main features are the Doric pilasters separating the tall arched windows and the huge segmental pediment with the clock in the tympanum. At the Grouping it became a joint LMS/LNER station. Grade II listed. (Photograph by Ben Brooksbank)

The original station at Tilbury Riverside was built in 1854. This was replaced by a new structure in 1924. Built in a Georgian style of gault brick, it has rusticated quoins and plinths and dressings of Portland stone. The station was used for the disembarkation of ocean-going liners, including the SS *Empire Windrush* in 1948. For this reason, and for the fact that the architect was Sir Edwin Cooper, the building is Grade II* listed. Passenger trains ceased calling in 1992.

South Eastern & Chatham Railway

The construction of the Medway Valley line by the South Eastern Railway in 1844–56 gave the opportunity for the construction of some remarkable stations. Wateringbury is a good example of 'railway Tudor', constructed in red brick with ashlar quoins, mullions and other decorative details. The windows have lozenge-shaped panes. 4-CEP unit No. 1530 arrives with the 15.03 Strood–Paddock Wood service on 27 June 1992. Grade II listed.

By contrast, further south is Yalding, nowadays simply a disused and bricked-up structure with a once elegant canopy, which unfortunately has been cut back to improve signal sighting. Note the various openings along the side of the platform which would have once accommodated the various levers, rods and wires of the signalling system.

North of Maidstone is Aylesford. Another 'railway Tudor' building, this time constructed of Kentish ragstone with Caen stone dressings, this building is Grade II listed. Once again we see lozenge-shaped windowpanes. An incongruous feature is the chimney stacks in buff brick, and there is also a decorative ridge crest.

This is Canterbury West, which was built for the SER in 1846. This simple classical design, typical of the mid-nineteenth century, is attributed to Samuel Beazley. A perfectly symmetrical stucco-faced building with a hidden roof and a deep cornice, it has a recessed entrance flanked by a pair of Doric columns and side pilasters. Grade II listed.

Wye, a station on the Ashford–Canterbury line, also opened in 1846. The station building consists of a three-storey gable and an adjoining single-storey structure, built of red brick with ashlar quoins and door and window dressings. It is vaguely Tudor in style. At the date of this photograph (1989) the station retained a signal box with semaphore signals and manually worked crossing gates. In fact, the signalman can be seen opening the gates after the passage of a train. The signal box was abolished in 2003 but the gates remain manually operated.

Appledore is a building of three bays with the centre gable set forward. It is constructed in red brick with pilasters and quoins in contrasting buff brick, with black brick footings. Designed by William Tress for the SER, its importance lies in the fact that it has remained almost completely unaltered since its construction in 1851. Grade II listed.

Westenhanger station was opened with the Ashford–Folkestone line in 1843, though the present structure dates from 1861. It is a rectangular building in buff brick with a string course in red. It has unusual corbelled eaves and sills and the chimney stacks are in red brick. In 1874 a branch to Hythe and Sandgate was opened. Passengers for this branch changed at Westenhanger.

Sandling station is a single-storey, timber-framed building with an infill of bricks in two different colours. The station was opened as Sandling Junction in 1888 to replace Westenhanger as the station for passengers for the Sandgate branch. This branch was cut back to Hythe in 1931 and closed completely in 1951.

The first station at Hastings was opened in 1851. This was replaced in 1931 by this striking art deco building by John Robb Scott. Despite its youth it was demolished in 2004 to make way for the present ultra-modern structure.

London, Brighton & South Coast Railway

The first station at Bexhill opened in 1846. Threatened by the new SECR branch line to Bexhill, which opened in 1902, the LB&SCR opened this new station. Designed by the company's chief engineer, Charles Morgan, it had a six-bay frontage with the centre four bays roofed by a pyramid leading to a glazed lantern with a bellcast roof. There is a scalloped canopy supported by four cast-iron columns across the whole frontage. Grade II listed.

Pevensey & Westham is one of a number of stations built by the LB&SCR in 1846 in a simple cottage style. It is a single-storey, stuccoed brick building with a central pediment. The rather nice canopy is supported on five slender cast-iron columns. The signal box is a Saxby & Farmer Type 5, built in 1876, and is a listed structure. It was taken out of use in 2015.

West Worthing was intended to be the terminus of a line from the Midlands to the south coast, but the line was never built. The present structure was built in 1889 to replace an earlier building. It is a stuccoed brick building of five bays, the three central being recessed, with two single-storey wings. Of note are the corbelled eaves, the window hood moulds and the unusual mouldings below the ground-floor windows.

The Mid Sussex line was completed in 1863, Arundel being the last station before the junction with the West Coast line. The station building has strong similarities with West Worthing – though, apart from window arches in contrasting red brick, it is much less embellished. While the main building is in English brick bond, for some curious reason the additional floor built onto one of the wings has been built in stretcher bond in different-coloured brick.

Amberley is the next station north on the Mid Sussex. A somewhat unprepossessing station, the main features to note are the canopy supported on wooden posts with splayed spandrels and the signal cabin dating from 1934, which was abolished in 2014. The line was electrified in 1938, leading to patronage almost doubling in ten years.

Leatherhead was built for the LB&SCR in 1867 to the design of Charles Driver. From 1927 it was shared with the Guildford line trains of the former LSWR. Built of brick with stone dressings, it consists of two pavilions joined by a central section fronted by a superb canopy supported on thin cast-iron columns. Grade II listed. (Photograph by Martyn Davies)

London & South Western Railway

The architect Sir Wiliam Tite did a lot of work for railway companies, including for the London & Southampton, as here at Micheldever. A simple and unfussy design of flint with quoins, dressings and plinth in buff brick. The canopy, supported on slender cast-iron columns, surrounds the whole building. Grade II listed, as is the telephone box.

Gosport is another work by Tite, and one of his best. Gosport, opened in 1841, was the original route to Portsmouth, which was reached by a ferry across the harbour. Portsmouth was not reached directly by rail until 1847. Gosport is a station in classical style, its most remarkable feature being the fourteen-bay Tuscan arcade in Portland stone. The station closed to passengers in 1953 and to freight in 1969. Some years ago a disastrous fire destroyed the roof. Grade II* listed. Also listed are the hexagonal 'Penfold' pillar box and the wall and iron railings (*see inset*), the latter thought to have been erected when Queen Victoria started to use the station when en route to the Isle of Wight.

Woolston is on the Southampton–Portsmouth line. A typical LSWR building of the mid-Victorian period, it is cement rendered with long and short quoins and a hipped slate roof, sitting on corbelled eaves. Note the unusual cut-out in the canopy, presumably to allow tall carriages to back up. Grade II listed.

Andover station opened in 1854. It became Andover Junction in 1865 with the arrival of the 'Sprat & Winkle line' from Redbridge. It was joined from the north by the Midland & South Western Junction Railway in 1882. This closed in 1961 and the 'Sprat & Winkle' in 1964, when the station became Andover once more. A 6-mile stretch of the M&SWJR survives to serve the MOD depot at Tidworth. The company GO-OP wishes to start a light-rail passenger service as far as Ludgershall.

Somewhat unusually the first railway to arrive at Salisbury was not from London but from Eastleigh in 1847. With the arrival of the Salisbury & Yeovil Railway a new station designed by William Tite was built. This is the building seen here, constructed of grey Fisherton brick with ashlar dressings and a slate roof. In 1901 a new station was built adjacent to the Tite station, and this is the building currently in use. Grade II listed.

Southampton Terminus is yet another Tite building, opened in 1840. This was the station for passengers taking transatlantic liners. It went out of use in 1966 and is now a casino. It is essentially a three-storey classical building, fronted by a five-arch rusticated loggia, above which sits a stone balustrade. Grade II listed.

The present Surbiton station, which has had a number of different names, including Kingston & Surbiton, and Kingston, was rebuilt in 1937 to the design of James Robb Scott. It is a superb example of 1930s art deco, sometimes referred to as 'Odeon style' due to the fact that many cinemas were being constructed at this time in the same style. Grade II listed. (Photograph by Steve Keiretsu)

The only noteworthy part of Waterloo station is the Victory Arch, built in 1919–22. Constructed of Portland stone, the bronze plaque under the arch lists the 585 employees of the LSWR who lost their lives in the First World War. The sculptures by Charles Whitten are, on the left, dedicated to Bellona, with the date 1914, and on the right to Peace, dated 1918. On the parapet is Britannia. Grade II listed. (Photograph by Perryman)

Great Western Railway

The present Reading station building dates from the period 1865–67 and was designed by Mr Lane, the GWR chief engineer. It is Italianate in style, built of buff brick with stone dressings and rusticated quoins. The first-floor windows have variously flat, segmental and pedimented hoods. The central section of the building has a corbelled cornice, surmounted by a strangely blank pediment. There is a rather nice clock turret. Grade II listed.

Pewsey dates from the opening of the Berks & Hants Extension Railway in 1862. Yet another example of 'railway Tudor', it is built of red brick, using bonds in a rather random fashion, and with ashlar quoins and dressings. There are some nice original features, including the shelter roof supported on wooden posts and a boot scraper adjacent to the waiting room door.

In 1856 the GWR branch from Westbury to Salisbury was opened and a Brunel-designed station was constructed adjacent to that of the LSWR. This is a single-storey brick building with stone dressings. It was closed to passengers in 1932 but continued as a goods shed, as seen in this 1990 photograph. It is now used as offices and is Grade II listed.

Details

At Kettering in 1989 was this early BR-era lamp standard with glass shades.

Also in 1989, at King's Cross, are these seemingly unwanted Type 60 hand barrows and a standard BR luggage trolley. With this type of trolley, the handle acted as a brake when in an upright position. More than one serious accident has been caused by allowing a trolley to roll onto the track.

The railway companies lost no opportunity to display their company monograms, as here on this GER bench at Worstead.

Somewhat more unusual are these 'serpent' benches at Goole.

These railings at Stallingborough are of a type common at GCR stations.

The LSWR pediment at Southampton Docks.

This clock at Canterbury West is marked BR (S). It is by John Walker of Molton Street, whose business is still at the same premises today.

A plaque at the GNR Retford station, which speaks for itself.

Elaborate spandrels supporting the canopy at Angmering.

The LB&SCR monogram in the ironwork of the roof at Hove.

Little remains of the Midland & Great Northern network. This spandrel is at Cromer.

Delivering the Goods

Major Goods Yards and Depots

As a guide to the quantity of goods once carried by the railways, one only has to look at the constant stream of lorries pounding up and down the motorways. At one time all these goods would have travelled by rail. Thus it was that the railway companies had need for such vast goods warehouses in major towns. Each railway company would have its own facilities, as here at Derby. This is the GNR Friargate depot, built 1877–78. Since this photograph was taken the building has undergone a significant deterioration, though it is Grade II listed.

The MR goods depot in Derby was at St Mary's. The building on the right is the goods shed, built *c.* 1861. It is of red brick with ashlar dressings. On the left is the granary, also dating from the early 1860s. It is an entirely symmetrical building and is also constructed of red brick. Both buildings are attributed to Thompson & Fryer and are Grade II listed.

King's Cross goods yard covered an area of 67 acres to the north of King's Cross station. This is the granary, which, like much else in the goods yard and King's Cross station itself, was designed by Lewis Cubitt. The whole goods yard has been redeveloped and the granary is now part of the University of the Arts. Grade II listed.

These are the coal drops at King's Cross. Wagons were shunted along these three tracks and coal dropped into the hoppers below. The railway tracks and the supporting arches have all been demolished, with the remaining buildings turned into a retail complex. Grade II listed.

One extraordinary part of the King's Cross goods yard was the potato market, seen here, which dealt with huge quantities of potatoes, especially during the harvest, when there might be a thousand wagons of potatoes waiting to be unloaded. In 1930 there were twenty-eight potato merchants occupying thirty-nine warehouses. The canopy was still remarkably complete in this 1989 photograph.

Another indication of the decline of rail freight. This is part of the complex of sidings at Glews Hollow at Goole Docks. Today, nothing remains here.

Perhaps not surprising that a brewing town like Burton-on-Trent should have such a large grain warehouse. An elegant and functional building now converted into a Travelodge hotel. The two-storey weather-boarded sack hoists survive in the redeveloped building. Grade II listed.

These are the GNR goods facilities at Nottingham London Road, seen in 1990. The building on the right is the granary, which has three-storey wooden sack hoists. The left-hand building also has hoists, supported on elegant curved brackets. These two buildings dramatically demonstrate the problem of buildings that are historically important but redundant. Despite being Grade II listed buildings, both are now roofless and in a derelict state.

The goods shed at Southampton was thought to have been designed by Sir William Tite. Of an unusual Gothic style, it is built of red brick with ashlar dressings. Described by Historic England as 'an early survival of a goods shed in a flamboyant style', this building is Grade II listed.

The rapid loss of general goods traffic led to thousands of goods sheds and depots becoming redundant almost overnight. The question was then what to do with them. Many were listed buildings, as here at the MR's Newark Castle goods shed. Happily, in this case a solution has been found in the form of conversion to offices. The main photograph was taken in 1989 and the inset in 1998. Grade II listed.

Medium-sized Goods Sheds

Broughton Lane station was a GCR station in the Sheffield area and it closed in 1956. Wooden goods sheds often failed to survive, either through fire, rot or simply being easy to demolish. Broughton Lane is an unusual type, with an entirely covered through road for vehicles. There is now a Sheffield Supertram stop at this location.

Burnham-on-Crouch is on the line to Southminster in Essex. This is also a building of an unusual type. Along the right-hand side at the two ends are cart docks where loading takes place from the shed via a platform, while the two centre docks allow ingress of vehicles.

The goods shed at Kirton Lindsey seems hugely out of proportion to the tiny settlement it serves, but agricultural areas generated huge amounts of business for the railways, mostly with the shipping of produce outward. The buildings have been much modified.

Saxilby is of the through type of shed, with a single cart dock covered with a canopy. The panelled walls and use of contrasting brick on the gable end and cornice give relief to an otherwise basic design.

Looking unloved in this photograph, the GNR goods shed at Retford has now found a new use as offices for Tarmac. This type of two-storey combined goods shed and warehouse was not uncommon. The small canopies above the sack hoists have been preserved in the refurbished building.

Arundel is another combined warehouse and goods shed. Its features include blind arches with lunette windows on both floors, a taking-in door within a blind arch beneath a gable on the upper floor and pilasters on either side of the two cart docks. Grade II listed.

Small Goods Sheds

This is the interior of Wellingborough goods shed in delightfully original condition, with its two wooden cranes held in place by cross members attached to the roof beams. The Gothic openings with typical MR lozenge-shaped windowpanes add to the charm. Grade II listed.

Another interior, this time at Goole. Track is still in place and the shed was being used by the civil engineering department. Here, the hand-worked crane is in steel.

Barnetby is a trackside goods shed; in other words, the wagons did not pass into the shed, as with larger buildings, but were shunted alongside. The canopy that protected the trackside operations can just be seen. On the opposite side is a single cart dock, also protected by a canopy.

Of a similar type is Ollerton, although here there are two cart docks. An unusual feature no longer extant is the canopy, which would have extended the full length of the building. The stone corbels that would have once supported the canopy can be clearly seen.

Despite its location alongside the East Coast Main Line, Helpston was in fact an MR granary. The passenger station closed in 1966 and no trace remains. The curved brackets supporting the overhanging eaves and the three sack hoists give the building considerable charm. Since this photograph was taken the granary has received a new roof and has been completely restored. Grade II listed.

Coal, Oil and Cattle

In 1993 the production of coal in British mines was in steep decline. Nevertheless, in that year 68 million tons was mined, almost all of it going to power-generating stations. Here we see No. 58036 with a train of merry-go-round hoppers being loaded at Bennerley Loading Point, alongside the Erewash Valley line.

This is Askern Colliery shortly after closure in December 1991. The last deep mine in Britain closed in 2015. In 2016 just 4 million tons of coal was mined in Britain and 8 million tons were imported. Most power stations now rely on burning biomass or gas.

Above and below: There was once a huge market for domestic coal. Every station would have had its coal merchant to whom supplies would be delivered by rail. Some locations had coal drops, like those shown here, where wagons would be shunted over the drops and coal was allowed to fall into the bins below. These drops were alongside the line at England Lane, near Knottingley.

At one time oil was another important traffic for rail. This is the oil terminal at Gainsborough Lea Road. This facility is now closed.

In 1961 British Railways still had nearly 5,000 cattle wagons, but this was a traffic in decline, and which had ceased altogether by the 1970s. However, before that decline each rural station would have its cattle pen where the livestock could be loaded directly into the cattle wagons. This example is at Braintree.

Equipment

Bulk goods needed to be weighed before leaving the goods yard and each station would have had a weighbridge, always accompanied by a weighbridge hut, which housed the equipment. At Spalding the weighbridge and its hut and equipment were still intact in 1989, when photographed.

For unloading heavy items in the yard many stations were equipped with a hand-worked crane, such as here at Essendine on the East Coast Main Line. The weighbridge hut can also be seen. Essendine station closed in 1959. It was near here in 1938 that Mallard broke the world speed record for steam.

Signalling and Signs

Signal Boxes

Possibly no other building is as characteristic of the railway as the traditional signal box. When BR took over the system in 1948 there were an estimated 10,000 signal boxes on the network. By 1970 this had declined to 4,000 and in 2015 there were just 373 mechanical boxes left. The eventual aim is for trains to be controlled from just fourteen signalling centres. The rapidly dwindling number of boxes has provoked considerable interest in recording, classifying and in some cases preserving signal boxes. Allington Junction, a GNR example dating from 1874, was not preserved, despite its great age. It was closed in 2005 and subsequently demolished.

In the early days much of the signalling of the railways was undertaken by contractors. It was only later that the railway companies themselves took over. Barrow Road Crossing box on the Barton-on-Humber branch was constructed by the Railway Signalling Company in 1885. It is a gate box with an eight-lever frame.

Godnow Bridge, on the Doncaster–Scunthorpe line, was another RSC box. This photograph dates from 1990. In 1998 the box was demolished and a new one was constructed in a similar 'period' style. It is no longer a block post and just controls a crossing.

Dinnington Colliery signal box was erected in 1912. It was a GCR Type 5. It sat at the junction of the GCR and MR joint line from Brancliffe Junction with the South Yorkshire joint line to Doncaster. The SYJ was a collaboration between no less than five railway companies: the GCR, GNR, MR, NER and L&Y. The box was abolished in 1998.

Yaxham is a GER Type 2 box dating from 1882. This line closed completely in 1969 but was later taken over by the Mid Norfolk Railway. The box is not functional as it no longer has its frame.

Above and below: This is Shippea Hill, a McKenzie & Holland GER Type 4 box dating from the 1880s. Characteristic of the Type 4 box was a door set in brickwork. Like many boxes in the Fens, Shippea Hill suffered from subsidence and it was abolished in 2012. The second photograph shows the thirty-lever McKenzie & Holland frame, together with the standard BR instruments.

The Midland Railway never used signalling contractors. In 1870 a signalling works was set up at Derby and the company from then on produced both its own frames and boxes. Almost without exception MR boxes were constructed of prefabricated wooden panels. The result is that MR boxes are unmistakable. There are very few early boxes and Totley Tunnel East is one of the earliest boxes still in use. It is a Type 2b and has a twelve-lever frame. It is due to be abolished in 2020.

Pinxton is another Type 2b and dates from 1897. It closed in 2007 and has been moved to Barrow Hill for preservation. Note that fixed to the Up starter signal (on the left) is a colour light signal. This is the Sleights East distant, which shows amber when the Pinxton home is pulled off, and green when Sleights home is pulled off. No. 58030 at the head of an empty MGR train sets off after a signal check.

Swinderby, on the Newark–Lincoln line, remains in use. It is a Type 3b dating from 1901 and is still equipped with its original sixteen-lever frame. A road that crosses the line diagonally has led to an odd gate solution, with a single gate on the right and a pair on the left. Grade II listed.

Another signal box still in use is Saltmarshe on the Hull–Goole line. The various divisions of the NER developed their own designs of signal box and Saltmarshe is classified as a Southern Type 2 (S2). It is a non-standard box, having a corner 'shaved off' in order to give the signaller a better view of the approaching traffic. It is due to be abolished in 2019.

This is the unique M&GN signal box at Cromer Yard. Dating from 1922, it is built of concrete blocks, although the front panels are faced with brick. It had a twenty-nine-lever frame, which was enlarged to thirty-five in 1954. The line on the left is to Norwich and that on the right goes to Sheringham, the last surviving vestige of the M&GN. The signal box was abolished in 2000. Since then it has been restored by the Cromer Railway Signalling Society and is open to the public. Grade II listed.

The signal box at Canterbury West was commissioned in 1928 and replaced two earlier SECR boxes. It has a standard SEC seventy-two-lever frame. It is one of the very few remaining boxes sited on gantries and is Grade II listed.

Wateringbury signal box is a Saxby & Farmer Type 12 box dating from 1893. It has a Duplex nine-lever frame, which is even older. Being largely unaltered it is the best preserved of its type. It has even been used as the basis for a Hornby model. Grade II listed.

The unimposing structure seen here is Grain Crossing box, which is Grade II listed. It is on the freight-only line to the terminal at Grain. Unimposing it may be, but it is historically important as it is the last surviving Stevens & Sons signal box in the country. Its low height is due to the fact that the locking room is below ground level. It dates from 1882 and is equipped with a nine-lever SER frame. Note the typical SR signal post made of two old rails.

Both John Saxby and John Farmer were former employees of the LB&SCR. It is not surprising then that so many of their signal boxes should be found on the system of their former employer. The Type 5 box, seen here at Warnham, was introduced in 1876 and continued to be produced for another twenty years or so. The box still has its original windows (though these were later replaced) and the signal post constructed of old rails, with a lattice post doll, was later replaced with a BR type.

A view of the twenty-lever frame at Warnham. Note the gate wheel. The box was abolished in 2005.

Further south on the Mid Sussex line is Pulborough, another Saxby & Farmer Type 5 box. Its external appearance is somewhat spoilt by the addition of a porch, but it is nevertheless an important survivor as it contains an almost complete set of original equipment, including its twenty-nine-lever LB&SCR frame. Grade II listed.

In the late 1930s the Southern Railway embraced the art deco style known as streamline moderne, somewhat more colloquially known as 'Odeon style'. The result was some very handsome buildings, including the signal box here at Templecombe, built in 1938. The box was closed in 2012 when the line was resignalled. Templecombe station itself closed in 1966, only to reopen in 1983.

Until 2000 Sloley Church Lane level crossing had a crossing keeper working this BR-pattern five-lever frame. In 1990 a Class 101 DMU heads past with a service for Sheringham. The crossing now has automatic half barriers.

Signals

These signals are for the Down main at Worksop West. The two subsidiary signals are for the reception sidings. Worksop West box was a MS&L Type 1, dating from 1874. It had a twenty-eight-lever frame and was abolished in 1998.

Langham Junction is between Melton Mowbray and Oakham on the Leicester–Peterborough line. It is at the start of the Up and Down goods loops. The right-hand signal controls entry to the Up goods loop. This photograph, taken in 1990, shows the lampman making his weekly visit to change the oil lamps that illuminated the signals aspects.

An identical pair of home signals at Sleaford West Junction. The left-hand signal controls exit from the Up and Down joint line, while that on the right is on the Nottingham line. Note the 'theatre' route indicators and the calling-on signals. The distant signals are operated by Sleaford East. These signals have now been replaced with coloured lights.

This is the Wainfleet Down distant. It is a Great Northern somersault signal. This type of signal was introduced after the Abbots Ripton accident, which was caused by a signal blocked by ice failing to return to danger. Notice the concrete signal post, a common feature of the GNR.

Wrawby was at the junction of the lines to Scunthorpe, Sheffield, Lincoln and Cleethorpes. This photograph was taken from the Lincoln line, looking towards the junction. This is a typical Great Central gantry. The taller signal is for the Up fast while the lower one is for the Up slow. The pair of subsidiary signals are for the reception sidings. The doll on the left was for the signal that controlled entry to the engine shed.

This photograph was taken from the other direction, again looking towards the junction. The three sets of signals are for the Down goods, the Down slow and the Down fast. In each case the left-hand signal is for the Lincoln line, the middle signal is for the Sheffield line and the right-hand signal is for the Scunthorpe line. Sadly this magnificent array is no more. The junction was resignalled in 2015 and is now controlled from York. The box survives as it is Grade II listed.

This is the Up starter signal at Cuxton on the Medway Valley line. The 'corrugated' signal on the left, of SR origin, gives access to the Up goods loop. The two dolls are typical LSWR lattice posts, although the left-hand one has lost its finial. Cuxton was resignalled with coloured lights in 2005 and the loop was abolished.

Another delightful relic from LSWR days is this gantry at the exit of Platforms 3 and 4 at Littlehampton. The signal arms and shunt signals are of BR origin. Sadly the lattice post dolls with their finials have now been replaced by conventional BR dolls, such as those seen on the other gantry at the exit to Platforms 1 and 2.

At Swanwick on the Midland Railway Centre preserved railway is this banner repeater. These were used when sighting was obscured to give the driver an advance indication of the signal.

Signs

This GCR sign at Reepham level crossing on the Lincoln–Barnetby line dates from the late nineteenth/early twentieth century. The MS&L changed its name to Great Central in 1897.

Grouping took place in 1923, when the GER became part of the LNER, thus dating this sign at King's Lynn to after that date. The sign could do with some attention to its English!

These two GNR signs were at Allington Junction, at the site of the now demolished signal box and level crossing. The use of cast iron by the pre-nationalisation companies gave a feeling of solidity and permanence.

This lovely cast-iron GNR sign at Ancaster on the Nottingham–Sleaford–Boston line also conveys a feeling of permanence.

Equally solid is this sign at Thornton Abbey on the New Holland/Barton line, consisting of cast-iron letters screwed onto a wooden base. In fact this line was one of those proposed for closure in the Beeching report. The eponymous abbey can be seen in the background.

The line to Littlehampton was electrified in 1938 and this enamel sign on the goods shed dates from that time.

Enamel signs were also favoured by the nationalised British Railways, which had different colours for its different regions – dark blue in the case of the Eastern Region. These enamel signs were replaced in the 1970s and 1980s to give BR more of a 'corporate' image, but a few survived in to the 1990s. This photograph was taken in 1993.

Temple Mills marshalling yard, in East London, received a huge modernisation in the 1950s. Sadly it was insufficient to save the kind of traffic it was meant to deal with. This photograph dates from 1989.

Indication of gradient was vitally important in the days of steam locomotives. At Elsham on the Doncaster–Barnetby line the gradient eases from 1 in 215 to 1 in 145. Note 'GCR' at the base of the post.

This somewhat less elaborate gradient post is at Buckenham on the Norwich–Lowestoft line.

The early railway companies were obliged by the government to erect mileposts in order to ensure that passengers were charged the correct fare. Of course, they were also extremely useful for the railway companies themselves. In the early part of the twentieth century the Midland Railway decided to re-milepost its network with a new type of milepost, an example of which is seen here at Linby. This milepost is 132¼ miles from St Pancras.

Another example of an MR milepost. The legend in the disc reads 'From K Jct', K in this case being Kingsbury. The distance is 0 miles because the milepost is at Kingsbury Junction itself.

This M&GN milepost is near Cromer on the preserved North Norfolk Railway.

Other Structures

Engine Sheds

At nationalisation in 1948 British Railways had some 20,000 steam locomotives and 689 loco sheds and depots in which to house and maintain them. The change from steam to diesel and electric led to a decreasing need for such depots, and while some continued to be used for the new modes of traction, the vast majority were simply abandoned, as here at Bedford. The depot was opened by the MR in 1868 and was closed by BR in 1963. Under BR it had the shed code 15D and later 14E.

This is the GNR shed at Lincoln. It closed to steam in 1964 but continued as a diesel depot, which accounts for its good condition when seen in 1991, shortly after closure. It had the code 40A. It has subsequently been rebuilt as a live music venue, perhaps unsurprisingly known as 'The Engine Shed'.

The roundhouse at Barrow Hill has had a long history. Known originally as Staveley, it was opened by the MR in 1870. Under BR it had the shed code 41E and after the end of steam it continued as a diesel depot, finally closing in 1991, shortly after this photograph was taken. It was taken over by the Barrow Hill Roundhouse and Railway Centre, opening to the public in 1998. Grade II listed.

Knottingley Traction Maintenance Depot was opened in 1967, specifically to maintain the diesel locomotives involved in the movement of coal to power stations. In this 1992 view a number of Class 56 and Class 08 locomotives can be seen. Today the depot is owned by DB Cargo and has an allocation of Class 60 and Class 66 locomotives.

Viaducts, Bridges and Tunnels

Digswell Viaduct is on the East Coast Main Line, just to the south of Welwyn North station. It is 1,560 feet long, 100 feet high, and consists of forty arches. It took two years to build. It was opened by Queen Victoria on 6 August 1850, though the queen, however, refused to travel across it. The structure is Grade II* listed.

A cast-iron bridge on the Bentinck Colliery line. The colliery closed in 1999 and the track has now been lifted.

On the preserved Churnet Valley Railway, 2-6-4T Standard tank No. 80136 crosses a steel girder bridge over the Caldon Canal. This bridge replaced an earlier arch bridge.

Designed by W. R. Galbraith for the LSWR, Kew Bridge was completed in 1869. It is a lattice girder bridge sitting on iron piers with engaged columns, each pier surmounted by an elaborate 'tabernacle'. Some of the piers have lost their engaged columns. Grade II listed. (Photograph by Edwardx)

The extraordinary north portal of Clayton Tunnel on the London–Brighton line of the LB&SCR, designed by David Mocatta. The 2,259-yard-long tunnel dates from 1841 but the cottage was added in 1849. This served as a wages office for a time and is now a private residence. Grade II listed. (Photograph by Cupcakekid)

Unlike Continental practice, in Britain passengers were not allowed to use board crossings to cross the tracks. Instead, subways, and more often footbridges, were provided. This superb example with wrought-iron latticework, cast-iron columns and sheet steel panelling is at March. Note also the canopy with its decorative valance.

In the 1890s the NER introduced a standard type of cast-iron footbridge. In some cases, as here at Goole, covering was provided.

At Sandling on the London–Folkestone line is this wrought-iron and steel footbridge set on cast-iron columns.

The concrete works at Exmouth Junction was founded by the LSWR and continued by the SR. A large range of prefabricated concrete products was produced, such as this footbridge at Wye. The components would arrive by train and then be craned into position. Note also the concrete lamp posts, another Exmouth Junction product, and the banner repeater signal mounted on a pair of old rails. On 10 April 1990, No. 47528 passes with a special train.

Crossing Cottages

From 1839 gates became mandatory at level crossings and accordingly a person had to be employed to operate the gates. In almost all cases a dwelling was provided for this person and his family. The crossing keeper's cottage seen here is on the part of the Hull & Barnsley Railway that was reused to give access to Drax Power Station.

This delightful lapped-boarded timber cottage is at Rackheath on the Norwich–Cromer line. It is painted in the green and cream colours so often favoured in ex-GER territory.

Manually operated crossing gates are increasingly rare. These massive gates are at Elsenham in Essex, where a minor road crosses the railway. Although minor, it is nevertheless busy and on a bend. While on duty, the crossing keeper is accommodated in the wooden hut.

Hotels

The Great Northern Hotel at King's Cross was designed by Lewis Cubitt, who was also the architect of King's Cross station. Built in 1854, it is of stock yellow brick with stucco dressings and has a dentilled cornice. Grade II listed.

The Midland Hotel at Derby was designed by Francis Thompson and completed in 1842. It is of red brick with stone dressings and quoins. The first-floor windows have stone balustrades. The square columns supporting the porch are matched by square chimney stacks. Grade II listed.

Lamps

For much of their history, the railways used oil lamps to illuminate stations and other buildings. Despite the arrival of electricity, and before that gas, this practice lasted well into the BR era. This elegant lamp used to illuminate the crossing at Stainton, on the Lincoln–Market Rasen line.

A structure found in many places was this rectangular bracket mounted on a wooden or concrete post. The bracket held the demountable oil lamp. This example is at the long-closed Boughton station on the Chesterfield–Lincoln line.

Other Buildings

Derby is a town of considerable historical interest as far as railways are concerned. It was the home of Derby Locomotive Works, established in 1839. The works closed in 1990 and most of it has now been demolished. The photograph shows the original North Midland workshops, which later became offices. As can be clearly seen, an extra storey was added in 1859–60, with the clock tower being raised at the same time. These buildings, the North Midland roundhouse and the Midland Counties workshops have been preserved and are Grade II* listed.

Also in Derby is the Railway Institute, opened in 1894 for the educational and recreational benefit of MR employees. It is interesting to compare the exuberant style of this late Victorian building with the more restrained design of the Midland Hotel. Now named Waterfall, it is an event venue.

The railway companies provided accommodation for the stationmaster at almost every station. This was not a philanthropic gesture as it meant that the stationmaster was on call twenty-four hours a day. Kegworth is a very fine example, constructed of red brick with stone dressings. Just discernible are the typical MR lozenge-shaped windows either side of the front door. The station itself closed in 1968.